BEFORE YOU TIE THE KNOT

Other resources by Dr. Angela Chester:

- *Before You Tie the Sacred Knot*
Premarital Counseling Workbook for the Christian Couple

My Life in Pink
A Collection of Survivor Stories

-*The Blueprint*
Designing A Successful Remarriage

BEFORE YOUTIE THE KNOT

A premarital counseling workbook
for the D.I.Y. couple

DR. ANGELA CHESTER

ANGELA CHESTER INTERNATIONAL

ANGELA CHESTER INTERNATIONAL

Before You Tie The Knot
A Premarital Counseling Workbook for the D.I.Y. Couple

This title is also available as an ebook.

Request for information should be mailed to:
Angela Chester International
110 West Ocean Boulevard, Suite 614 Long Beach, CA 90802

ISBN 978-1-304-29698-6

Printed in the United States of America

Contents

How To Use This Workbook

Group Size

The *Before You Tie The Knot* workbook is designed to be experienced in a couples setting. To ensure everyone has enough time to participate in discussion, it is recommended that you spend sixty minutes total on each session.

Materials Needed

- Workbooks
- Pen / Pencil
- Timer

Each participant should have his or her own workbook. This ensures that each participant regarding the other person makes proper notes.

Timing

The timing notations – for example (30 minutes) – indicate the suggested times for each activity.

Session 1: Relationships

This section should take 60 minutes.

Take a moment to answer the following questions. Sometimes you may feel your answer needs an explanation – use the percentage option.

Core Values

1. Do you feel your fiancé(e) is an honest and truthful person? ☐Yes ☐ No ☐ ____% of the time

2. Do you feel you can trust your fiancé(e)?
☐Yes ☐ No ☐ ____% of the time

3. Do you feel your fiancé(e) loves and respects you? ☐Yes ☐ No ☐ ____% of the time

4. Do you believe your fiancé(e) will be faithful?
☐Yes ☐ No ☐ ____% of the time

5. Do you see yourselves growing old together?
☐Yes ☐ No ☐ ____% of the time

6. Is your fiancé(e) understanding of your family?
☐Yes ☐ No ☐ ____% of the time

Physical Attraction

7. Why are you attracted to your fiancé(e)?

8. What do you think attracts your fiancé(e) most to you?

Emotional Basics

9. Is it hard to say "thank you" or "please" or "I'm sorry" to your fiancé(e)? If so, why?

10. When you are not feeling well, how much sympathy and attention do you feel you need? Use scale 0-10. Explain.

11. How do you show affection to your fiancé(e)?

12. Do you think this form of affection is pleasing to him/her, or it is all you can give?

☐Yes ☐ No ☐ All I can give

13. Are your fiancé(e)'s signs of affection sufficient for you? If not why:

____
____
____
____
____
____
____
____

14. Is your fiancé(e) kind, gentle and understanding? How do you feel about that?

____
____
____
____
____
____
____
____
____
____
____
____
____

15.. Do you often use the words “Always” or “Never” during a disagreement?

☐Yes ☐ No ☐ ____% of the time

16. Which word(s) best describes when you don’t see eye to eye: *(check all that apply)*

☐ Fight
☐Disagreement
☐Misunderstanding
☐Debate
☐Miscommunication
☐Dip
☐Time Out
☐Argument
☐Squabble
☐Spat
☐Bicker
☐Temporary Setback

The In-Laws

17. Will your parents be living with you?

☐Yes ☐ No ☐ ____% of the time

How do you feel about that?

____

____

____

18. Will your fiancé(e)s parents be living with you?

☐Yes ☐ No ☐ ____% of the time

How do you feel about that?

____

____

____

____

19. Do you like your future In-laws?

☐Yes ☐ No ☐ ____% of the time

Because…

____

____

____

____

____

____

____

____

____

____

____

20. Do you feel your future In-laws like you?

☐Yes ☐ No ☐ ____% of the time

Because…

____

____

____

____

____

____

____

____

____

People

21. Will you continue to have contact with old friends of the opposite sex? ☐Yes ☐ No

22. Will new friends of the opposite sex be "allowed" in your marriage? ☐Yes ☐ No ☐ ____% of the time

Because…

____
____
____
____
____
____
____
____

23. Will your contact with opposite sex friends on Facebook, Twitter (any social networking site) be acceptable? ☐Yes ☐ No ☐ ____% of the time

Because…

____
____
____
____
____
____
____

24. How do you feel about phone calls (cell phone or landline) after 10 p.m.?

25.How do you feel about the cell phone being on vibrate?

26. Will your fiancé(e) have access to PINs for email, cell phone, etc..?

☐Yes ☐ No

Because…

Standpoint

27. What type of spouse do you see yourself being? Why is this important to you?

28. What words best describe the perfect spouse for you? Why is this important to you?

Decision Making

29. How will you make day-to-day decisions once you are married?

30. How will you make major decisions once you are married?

31. How will you handle end of life decisions?

32. Who has the final word when a mutual decision can't be reached? Why?

33. The Scenario:

(A) You can't come to an agreement on point X. The final decision maker has decided, however, you disagree. The final outcome of point X is a positive one. How do you feel about the outcome?

(B) The Scenario:

You can't come to an agreement on point X. The final decision maker has decided, however, you disagree. The final outcome of point X is a negative one. More issues are now added to the original issue.

How do you feel about the outcome?

34. Do you past relationship "junk"

☐Yes ☐ No ☐ ____% of the time

35. Which of these issues need the most attention?

36. Is there anything you'd change about your fiancé(e)? Why is that important to you?

36. Is there anything you'd change about yourself? Why is that important to you?

What have you learned about your fiancé(e)?

What have you learned about yourself?

Session 2: Education & Career

This section should take 20 minutes.

Education

1. Is your fiancé(e)'s education level an issue of concern for you? ☐Yes ☐ No ☐ ____% of the time

Because…

____

____

____

____

____

____

____

____

2.Is your level of education an issue of concern for you? ☐Yes ☐ No ☐ ____% of the time

Because…

____

____

____

____

____

____

____

3. What are your career goals?

____
____
____
____
____
____
____
____

4. What are your fiancé(e)'s career goals?

____
____
____
____
____
____
____
____

5. How do your goals fit with your fiancé(e)'s hopes & dreams for the future?

____
____
____
____
____
____
____

Note

What have you learned about your fiancé(e)?

What have you learned about yourself?

Session 2: Sexual Outlook

This section should take 20 minutes.

Expectations

1. How often is "*often*" when it comes to being intimate? Why do you think this is reasonable?

____

____

____

____

____

____

____

2. Do you need to cuddle before being intimate? Does your fiancé(e)?

☐Yes ☐ No ☐ ____% of the time

3. Does your fiancé(e) need to cuddle before being intimate?

☐Yes ☐ No ☐ ____% of the time

4. What do you consider "cuddling" to be?

____

____

____

____

5. Do you need to “set the mood” to get in the mood?

☐Yes ☐ No ☐ ____% of he time

6. If you and your fiancé(e) have been in an argument, do you still feel sexy?

☐Yes ☐ No ☐ ____% of he time

What have you learned about your fiancé(e)?

What have you learned about yourself?

Happy Marriage Notes

Things I do can do to keep the happiness ...

Happy Marriage Notes

… and things I can to *change* to make it happier

Session 3: Finances

This section should take 40 minutes.

Credit

1. Have you discussed your credit with your fiancé(e)?

☐Yes ☐ No

2. Are you familiar with your credit score?

☐Yes ☐ No ☐ Some Idea

Expectations

3. Who will be the primary financial provider for the family?

☐Husband ☐ Wife

4. Will the wife work outside the home or be a housewife/mother?

☐Housewife ☐ Outside work

5. Who will be the primary accountant / record keeper?

☐Husband ☐ Wife

6. Which will you have?

- Checking Account

☐Joint ☐Personal ☐Both ☐None

- Savings Account

☐Joint ☐Personal ☐Both ☐None

7. How should bill payments occur?

☐Online ☐In Person ☐Mail

8. Do you balance your checkbook on a daily basis?

☐Yes ☐ No ☐ ____% of the time

9. Once married, who will balance the checkbook?

☐Husband ☐ Wife ☐ Both

10. As an individual - did you have a written budget?

☐Yes ☐ No ☐ ____% of the time

11. As a couple - have you created a family budget?

☐Yes ☐ No ☐ ____% complete

Budget

12. What percentage of your income will go towards home, car, groceries, bills, etc.?

☐75% ☐ 65% ☐50% ☐ 30%

13. What percentage of your income will go towards savings?

☐75% ☐ 65% ☐50% ☐ 30%

14. Have you created an "emergency fund" or a "rainy day" account?

☐Yes ☐ No ☐ ____% of goal

15. Do you have a retirement fund (401k, IRA, etc.)?

☐Yes ☐ No

16. If you have children – do they have/plan to have a college fund or trust?

☐ n/a ☐ 529 ☐ Trust ☐ Both

17. Once married, would you seek the advice of a financial planner?

☐Yes ☐ No ☐ Currently use

18. How do you feel about credit cards?

____

____

____

____

19.If either you or your spouse lost a job, what budget items would you cut?

____

____

Giving

20. What is your philosophy on giving to charitable organizations?

____

____

21. Will you tithe or support a local church/temple/house of worship?

☐Yes ☐ No

22. What percentage of your income will go towards giving?

☐35%+ ☐ 25% ☐10% ☐ 5% ☐ <3%

What have you learned about your fiancé(e)?

What have you learned about yourself?

Session 4: Home & Housekeeping

This section should take 20 minutes.

Outlook

1. What living style fits you best?

- ☐ City
- ☐ Suburbs
- ☐ House
- ☐ Condo
- ☐ Mountains
- ☐ Beach

2. What do you expect your standard of living to be immediately after you are married?

____

____

____

____

____

3. What do you expect your standard of living to be one year after you are married?

____

____

____

____

____

4. What do you expect your standard of living to be 5 years after you are married?

____

____

____

5. Five years later: Your standard of living as not been achieved. How do you think that will make you feel?

____

____

____

____

____

6. How soon after you are married, do you expect to have your home reasonably furnished?

____

____

____

____

____

____

7. How important are home trends to you?

☐ I'm a trendsetter / makes changes often

☐ Change accessories according to season

☐ Purchase only the basics

☐ Using inherited furniture

Because…

____

____

____

____

____

Expectation

8. Will you do your own home maintenance and gardening, or have a service / vendor do this for you?

☐ Myself ☐ Hire ☐ Included

9. What type of food will you eat and who will prepare each dish?

____

____

____

10. How often will you dine out?

☐ Daily

☐ Weekly

☐ Monthly

☐ Special Occasions

11. Who will pay for the meals when you dine out?

☐ Husband ☐ Wife ☐ Both

12. Who will do the laundry and ironing?

☐ Husband ☐ Wife ☐ Both

13. Who will be the main grocery shopper?

☐ Husband ☐ Wife ☐ Both

14. Who attends to car maintenance?

☐ Husband ☐ Wife ☐ Both

15. Who will do general household cleaning and bed making?

☐ Husband ☐ Wife ☐ Both

16. Who is the main dishwasher (hand wash or load machine)?

☐ Husband ☐ Wife ☐ Both

17. Will you own a pet? ☐ No ☐ Yes

a) What type?

____

b) Who will tend to the pet on a daily basis?

☐ Husband ☐ Wife ☐ Both

18. If the main food preparer works outside the home, and he/she prepares dinner, what time do you expect to eat and why:

____

____

____

____

____

____

19. If the main food preparer works within the home and he/she prepares dinner, what time do you expect to eat?

____

____

20. Do you expect to go out to eat for your birthday or special holidays / events?

☐ No ☐ Yes ☐ Only if in the budget

21. Is ordering out for dinner the same as preparing it yourself?

☐ No ☐ Yes

Because…

____

____

____

22. Who will have the longest "honey-do" list? *(list of things to do around the house)*

☐ Husband ☐ Wife

23. You've agreed to do a certain task, your fiancé(e) does it for you. How does that make you feel?

____

____

____

24. Has your fiancée expressed a dislike for housework?

☐ No ☐ Yes ☐ Sometimes

25. What are your “big picture” expectations about your home life?

26. Which of your family’s traditions do you wish to bring into your married life?

27. What new traditions would you like to make part of your married life?

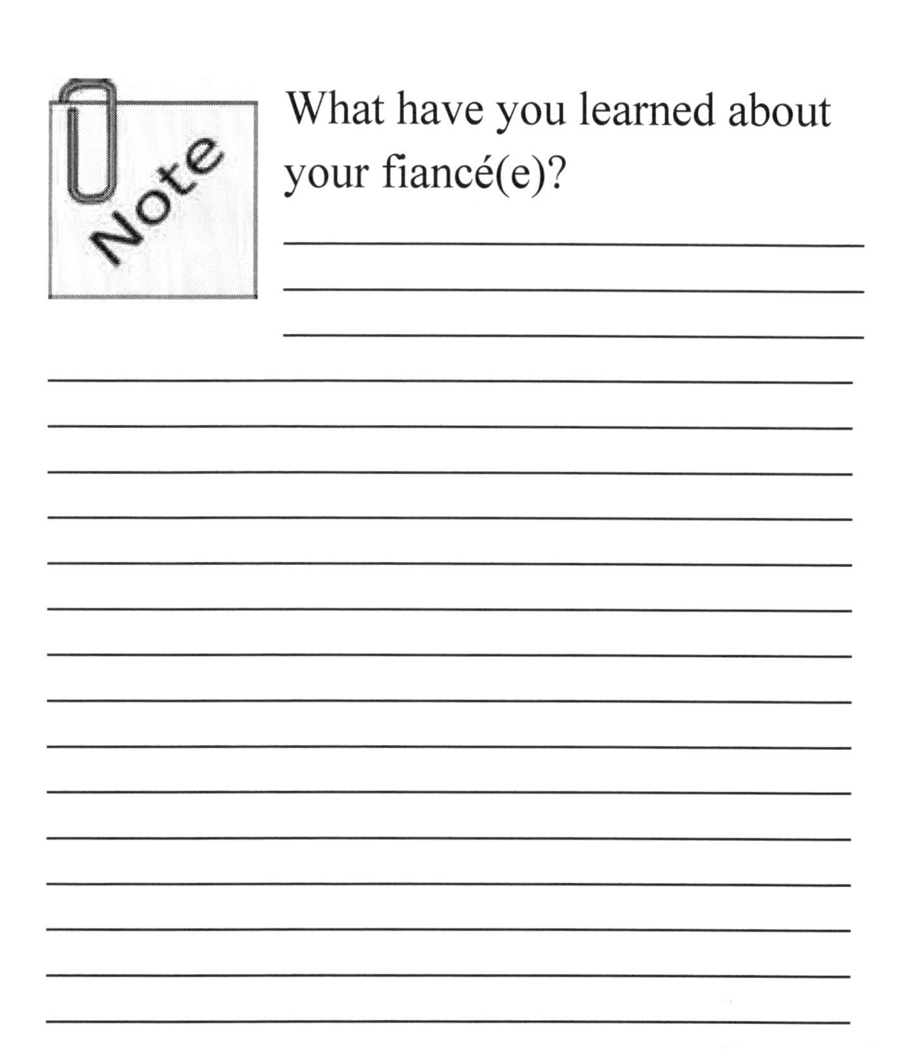

What have you learned about your fiancé(e)?

What have you learned about yourself?

Session 5: Children & Parenting

This section should take 60 minutes.

Outlook

1. What's your attitude towards children?

☐ Love 'em ☐ No kids

Because…

____

____

____

____

____

2. Have any children been lost due to death? How are you dealing with it?

____

____

____

____

____

____

____

3. How soon after the wedding will you begin planning for children?

____

____

4. How many children do you wish to have?

☐ 1 ☐ 2 or 3 ☐ ±4 ☐ No limit

5. What will you do if you cannot conceive children?

____

____

____

____

6. Are you ☐ProLife or ☐ProChoice

Because…

____

____

____

7. What is your view on birth control?

____

____

____

8. Does your fiancé(e) share your view on birth control? ☐ Yes ☐ No

Because…

____

____

____

____

Parenting Style

9. Will your children have a bedtime?

☐ Yes ☐ No *What time…*

____

10. Sleeping arrangements / where will the children sleep:

☐ Alone only ☐ With you (community bed) ☐ Both

Because…

____

____

____

____

11. Who will be the primary caregiver for the children?

☐ Husband ☐ Wife

12. What form(s) of discipline will you use for the children?

____

____

Because…

____

____

____

____

13. Who will be the primary disciplinarian? ☐ Husband ☐ Wife

14. Will your children have chores?

☐ Yes ☐ No *What age…*

____

____

____

15. Will your children receive an allowance; How much and how often?

____

____

____

16. At what age will your children be allowed to have social networking pages (Facebook, Twitter, etc.)?

☐ 8-9 yrs. ☐ 10-12yrs. ☐ 13+ yrs.

Because…

____

____

17. What age is appropriate to have a cell phone?

☐ 8-9 yrs. ☐ 10-12yrs. ☐ 13+ yrs.

Because…

____

____

18. How much time will be allowed on the computer?

☐ 30 – 90 mins. ☐ 2-3 hrs. ☐ No limit

19. Will you require the password to:

a) Social network pages ☐ Yes ☐ No

b) Any computers ☐ Yes ☐ No

c) Cell phone ☐ Yes ☐ No

20. What areas will you impose boundaries for your children?

____

____

____

____

____

____

____

____

____

____

____

____

21. How long will your children be allowed to live at home?

____

____

____

____

22. If you already have children, will they be living with you?

☐ Yes ☐ No ☐ Co-parent

23. Will that affect your day-to-day schedule in anyway?

____

____

____

24. How will you deal with school issues and events?

____

____

____

____

25. Do you get along with the birth parent? ☐Yes ☐ No ☐ ____% of the time

Because…

____

____

____

26. What is your philosophy on step- vs. half- vs. whole (birth) status?

____

____

____

27. Do your family members share your philosophy on birth status? If not, how will that affect your children?

____

____

____

____

28. What will any stepchildren call their stepparent. Why?

____

____

____

29. Do your birth children have any issues with your fiancé(e)?

☐ No ☐ Yes

Because…

____

____

30.What do you do to encourage or remedy the situation?

____

____

____

____

____

____

____

31. How do you feel about adult children living with you?

32.Does your fiancé(e) feel the same way?

☐ No ☐ Yes

Because…

33. If you don't agree, what is your compromise?

What have you learned about your fiancé(e)?

What have you learned about yourself?

Session 6: Social Activities

This section should take 30 minutes.

The Basics

1. Do you share the same beliefs / are you the same faith?

☐Yes ☐ No ☐ ____% of the time

2. Do you attend the same temple / house of worship / church?

☐Yes ☐ No ☐ ____% of the time

3. After marriage, will you attend the same house of worship?

☐Yes ☐ No ☐ ____% of the time

4. Will you share your faith with your children?

☐ No ☐ Yes

Because…

____

____

____

5. Will you continue any hobbies you have once married?

☐Yes ☐ No ☐ ____% of the time

6. Will you continue your recreational schedule once married?

☐Yes ☐ No ☐ ____% of the time

7. Will you start any new hobbies or recreational activities once your are married?

☐Yes ☐ No ☐ Probably not

8. Are you willing to participate in activities to solely please your fiancé(e)? Which ones?

☐Yes ☐ No ☐ ____% of the time

9. Will your personal friendships change after marriage?

☐ Stay the same ☐ Will change

Because...

____

____

____

____

10. How do you feel about alcoholic beverages, smoking and guns in your home?

____

____

____

____

____

11. Where will you spend the holidays, birthdays and anniversaries?

Holidays____

____

____

____

_

Birthdays____

____

____

____

Anniversaries_____________________________________

____

____

____

12. Will you be joining any new social clubs?

☐Yes ☐ No ☐ Maybe

13.Have you included a date night?

☐Yes ☐ No ☐ Planning stages

What have you learned about your fiancé(e)?

What have you learned about yourself?

- Adjustment for a happier marriage

Session 7: Red Flags

This section should take 30 minutes.

The Basics

1. Does your fiancé(e) seem to be irrationally jealous of friends, family or past relationships?

☐Yes ☐ No ☐ ____% of the time

2. Is your fiancé(e) prone to extreme emotional outbursts and / or very bad mood swings?

☐Yes ☐ No ☐ ____% of the time

3. Does your fiancé(e) display controlling behavior?

☐Yes ☐ No ☐ ____% of the time

4. Is your fiancé(e) unable to hold a job for any length of time?

☐Yes ☐ No ☐ ____% of the time

5. Are you unable to resolve your conflict?

☐Yes ☐ No ☐ ____% of the time

6. Does your fiancé(e) tell lies for no reason?

☐Yes ☐ No ☐ ____% of the time

7. Does your fiancé(e) treat you with respect?

☐Yes ☐ No ☐ ____% of the time

8. Does your fiancé(e) humiliate you in public often?

☐Yes ☐ No ☐ ____% of the time

9. Does your fiancé(e) like to gossip?

☐Yes ☐ No ☐ ____% of the time

10. Does your fiancé(e) embellish about your relationship?

☐Yes ☐ No ☐ ____% of the time

11. Is your fiancé(e) overly dependent on others for money?

☐Yes ☐ No ☐ ____% of the time

12. Do you feel your fiancé(e) abuses you sexual?

☐Yes ☐ No ☐ ____% of the time

13. Does your fiancé(e) abuse you physically?

☐Yes ☐ No ☐ ____% of the time

14. Does your fiancé(e) abuse you emotionally?

☐Yes ☐ No ☐ ____% of the time

15. Does your fiancé(e) constantly call you names / put you down?

☐Yes ☐ No ☐ ____% of the time

16. Does your fiancée abuse alcohol or drugs?

☐Yes ☐ No ☐ ____% of the time

- Adjustment for a happier marriage

Made in the USA
Lexington, KY
06 January 2019